# SMART GREEN CIVILI

# ANCIENT AMERICA

teri

The Energy and Resources Institute

## A note from Dr R K Pachauri

Human civilization in its race towards progress has at times ignored its adverse effects on nature. With every passing century, man has intensified his quest for a tomorrow better than today, and issues like environment-friendly living, usage of clean energy and preventing the harmful effects of chemicals on nature are becoming increasingly important. Contrary to popular belief, these can be tackled without compromising on our comforts. All we need to do is turn a few pages of history and relearn lessons that civilizations from various parts of the world have left behind.

This series provides a unique and interesting perspective of history from the eyes of an environmentalist. It highlights the environmental wisdom of ancient people. These books bring alive ancient civilizations and their simple, earth-friendly lifestyles—building bright and airy houses from mud bricks, using the sun's energy to heat homes, utilizing plants to make natural dyes, applying manure to grow crops, and many more such techniques.

Exploring the fascinating civilizations of the ancient world and bringing forth little known 'green lessons' from the past, I hope these books will ensure that young readers put to use the knowledge of yesteryears to lay the foundation for a prosperous future.

R K Pachauri
Director-General, TERI
Chairman, Intergovernmental Panel on Climate Change

# Contents

# Teri and the Maya mask

This will be a good outfit for my costume party!

Uh, oh... where am I?

W-H-O-O-S-HHHH

That's a magic Maya mask...it is taking you to a fascinating land of corn, colour, and chocolate!

Around 2600 BC, groups of people are believed to have settled in Central and South America. These were the Maya, Inca, Aztec, and Olmec. Together, these people formed what is called the Mesoamerican civilization. The Maya had the largest settlement.

The Mesoamerican groups were settled close to each other, and so, they had a lot in common. They are known for their writing, art and architecture, and grand buildings. While the Maya were not the first in the region to begin writing, they improved on what they learnt from their neighbours.

The ancient Maya lived in an area that stretched from the mountains of Sierra Madre to the plains of Yucatan. Today, this land comprises the countries of Mexico, Guatemala, Belize, and Honduras. The earliest Maya settlements were along the Pacific coast, dating back to around 1800 BC. The best or classic period was between AD 250 and AD 900, when cities and settlements flourished across the region. There were independent regions called city states.

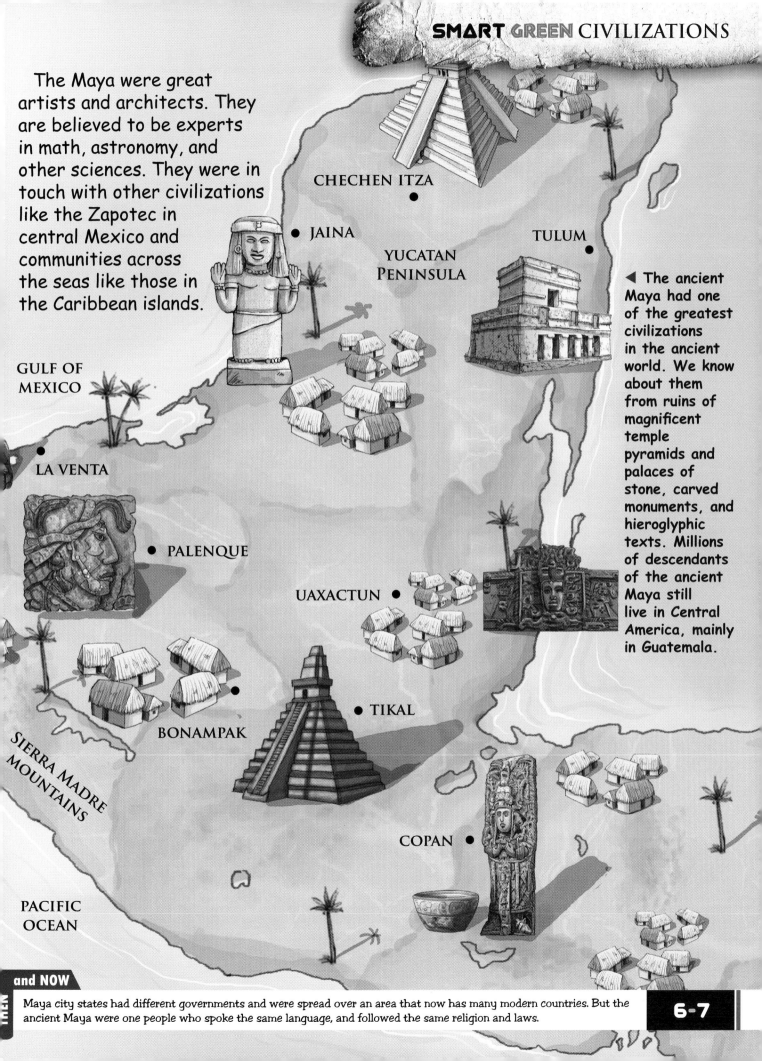

The Maya were great artists and architects. They are believed to be experts in math, astronomy, and other sciences. They were in touch with other civilizations like the Zapotec in central Mexico and communities across the seas like those in the Caribbean islands.

CHECHEN ITZA •

JAINA •

YUCATAN PENINSULA

TULUM •

GULF OF MEXICO

◄ The ancient Maya had one of the greatest civilizations in the ancient world. We know about them from ruins of magnificent temple pyramids and palaces of stone, carved monuments, and hieroglyphic texts. Millions of descendants of the ancient Maya still live in Central America, mainly in Guatemala.

• LA VENTA

• PALENQUE

UAXACTUN •

• BONAMPAK

• TIKAL

SIERRA MADRE MOUNTAINS

COPAN •

PACIFIC OCEAN

**and NOW**

Maya city states had different governments and were spread over an area that now has many modern countries. But the ancient Maya were one people who spoke the same language, and followed the same religion and laws.

Uh, oh... Where am I?

Welcome to the land of the ancient Maya. I am Itzel, and I will be happy to show you my civilization.

# People and society

The Maya divided themselves into classes. At the head was the ruler—almost always a man. He was surrounded by priests and nobles. Then, there were soldiers and traders. Below these were craftsmen and artists, who made huge statues and stone carvings. The rest of the people were mostly farmers. Slaves worked hard in the fields or in the homes of nobles.

The Maya civilization grew around city states that had one capital city and a few small towns around it. Each city was ruled by a different family. The father handed the responsibility of governing the city to his son, so power stayed with one family. The Maya believed that their rulers descended from the Hero Twins, whom they worshipped. The royal family lived in a palace. Since there was just one ruling family, most cities had just one palace.

▼ At the top of the Maya society was the powerful king of the city state and his family, as well as nobles and priests. Sometimes, the king performed the duties of a priest.

▼ Below the rulers were artists, architects, scribes, traders, and farmers.

▼ The lowest class were the slaves. Slaves were caught during wars. People who were caught committing a crime also became slaves.

The Yucatan Peninsula was dry. The Maya caught rainwater in chaltunes, or tanks lined with plaster.

The nobles were related to the ruler. They advised the ruler on how to run the city. When the nobles came out of their homes, servants held a cloth in front of their face to keep them shielded from common people.

The Maya city states often fought among themselves. This meant that soldiers were important people. Before they went to battle, soldiers made their own shields decorated with pictures of all their victories. Those who lost were taken away as slaves. Farmers worked hard to grow food for themselves and for their rulers, nobles, and soldiers.

▼ The Maya had markets where artisans sold pottery, baskets, and other handicraft.

and NOW

The Maya did not have metal tools but they used the crystal obsidian, which is harder than steel, to make things they needed to build their cities.

8-9

# Growing food

A new civilization can thrive only if people grow their own food. The Maya were able farmers who grew enough to feed their people and more. They perfected the raised bed method of farming, where permanent raised fields were connected by canals. This made it simpler to water fields and made sure excess water ran down to the next field. Although they did not know how to use metal tools for a long time, they used stone axes and their bare hands.

Mmm...delicious!

Corn was special...a gift from the gods.

▼ The ancient Maya developed different methods of growing crops, like the permanent raised fields connected by canals. Modern Maya people still practise many of these traditional forms of farming.

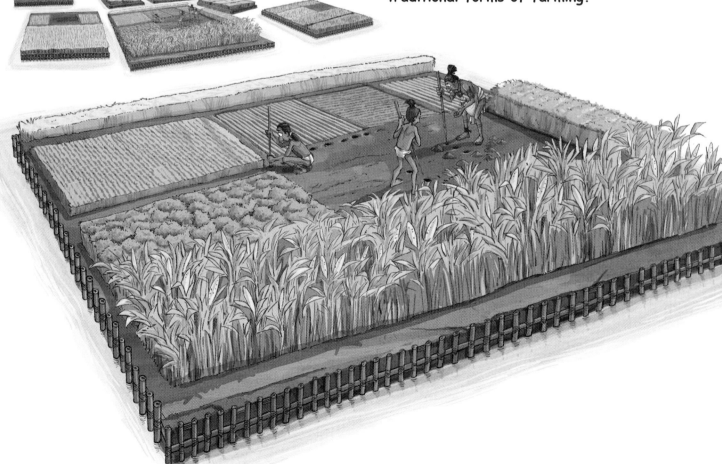

Where the land was forested, Maya farmers used the slash-and-burn method. They cut trees where they needed to farm and burnt down the stubs of trees to make a field, or milpa. The ashes that mixed with the soil made the land more fertile. But repeated crops robbed the land of nutrients. So, after a few years, the farmers moved on to new areas. Some fields were permanent.

Farmers grew corn and cacao and vegetables like beans, squash, and peppers. They cultivated sisal and cotton for thread. They also grew manioc, a woody shrub commonly grown in South America for its starchy root.

In marshy areas, farmers scooped out the soggy soil rich in natural goodness and made beds of it. No land was too arid. Maya farmers knew how to convert fallow land into fields. In the hills, they cut terraces. This made it easier to grow crops on slopes and helped catch rainwater to feed the plants. It was also a good way to keep the soil from washing away.

◀ Maya farmers used simple tools that made their work easier and improved the quality of their crops.

▶ Corn was the most important crop of the Maya. It grew easily and in plenty and so, it landed up in the kitchen for every meal.

and NOW

THEN

Even today, some Maya use the techniques of their ancient ancestors to grow crops.

10-11

# At home with the Maya

Is this tea or coffee?

It's chocolate; we had it for breakfast, lunch, and dinner!

If you could visit a Maya village, you would find women and girls at home. Generally, men were farmers and women helped when they needed more hands. Boys helped their fathers on the field. While the men were away in the fields, women cleaned the house, cooked, spun and wove cotton, and stitched and embroidered clothes. The women also carried back grain from the fields in baskets and to sell in the market.

▶ The Maya hunted animals and birds like macaws, turkeys, and ducks for food. They used every part of the animal for food, clothing, and tools.

Corn was so important to the Maya that they considered it holy. Some nobles tied their hair to look like corn!

▲ The Maya family lived together. The women would cook and weave, while the men farmed and hunted. Children helped their mother with household chores. Only children from noble families went to school.

The Maya ate wholesome food. Since corn grew in plenty, even peasants ate corn. It was made into gruel for breakfast and pancakes called tortillas for other meals. They ate vegetables like beans, chillies, sweet potatoes, and squash. Men caught fish and hunted deer. They used blow-pipes to bring down wild ducks and turkey. They also laid traps for prey. From the earlier Olmec civilization, they learnt to dry, roast, and grind cacao beans to make a chocolate drink, which they poured out of a spouted ceramic pot. The scientific name of the cacao plant is *Theobroma cacao*. It means 'food of the gods'. Although common people also drank chocolate, the Maya believed it was a food for the rulers and gods.

The Maya loved music and dance. They performed hundreds of dances in bright costumes and large headgear to drum beats. Their dances were a tribute to nature and so, they had the centipede dance and the monkey dance. Musicians played wooden flutes, rattles, shell horns, and castanets.

**and NOW**

The ancient Maya liked their chocolate drink thick and frothy. They would have been disappointed to see the thin chocolate we drink!

# Architecture and cities

Such heavy stones...where are the machines to cut them?

You'll be surprised to know, we hardly had any tools, and we worked with our hands!

The Maya were expert builders. When you see their pyramids, carved caves, and temples you would never guess they did not know how to make metal tools. Nor did they use animals to draw carts of construction material. They did not even have pulleys to lug heavy material up the slopes. They relied on human hands and used local material like stone, as it could be used where it was mined. They found that limestone was soft and could be carved when it was freshly quarried. Bricks were cemented with burnt limestone mortar.

**GREEN GEM** As time went by, the workers became experts at cutting the stones to fit perfectly without any mortar, specially in larger buildings like temples. So, no mortar was wasted.

Important cities of the Maya included Tikal, Copan, and Palenque. Each city was built around a market and had a public courtyard, or plaza, where people met. The centre of the city had the palace, decorated with carvings, and pyramids with temples atop them to signify being close to heaven. In a land covered by towering jungles, these were landmarks that rose above the trees.

Below the pyramid was a ball court with stadium seating. Beyond the palace were houses of nobles and smaller shrines. On the outskirts were thatched homes of common people. Good roads stretched for miles, connecting cities.

Cities had public platforms for ceremonies. Since the Maya were fascinated by the stars, they built observatories to study the movement of the planets. One such observatory is at Uaxactun.

▲ Though the Maya did not lack materials like stone and limestone, they did not have tools and technologies for huge constructions. Building the cities and buildings needed a lot of manpower.

◀ Maya cities usually had huge temple pyramids, palaces, and houses built on stepped platforms. These buildings were arranged around broad plazas, or courtyards.

**and NOW**
The ancient Maya held religious rituals in caves called Jolja and Candelaria and decorated them with mural paintings and carvings. The Maya still use some of these caves for ceremonies.

# Maya attire

The land of the Maya had a hot climate, so people wore clothes made of cotton or rough sisal fibre. Only kings wore skirts of jaguar skin. In everyday life, men wore a breechcloth. Over that, they often wore a shirt. Women wore the colourful huipil blouse and an ankle-long wrap skirt, or corte. It was tied at the waist with a belt, or faja. The manta, a large piece of cloth, was used as a wrap in colder weather. When someone was not wearing the manta, it was used as a curtain.

◄ The Maya were known for their skilled weaving and bright colours. This ancient art has survived over the ages to become famous all over the world.

Cloth was woven by women who knew beautiful weaving techniques. As in most other civilizations, the priests and the rich wore finer and more beautiful clothes, while poor farmers wore plain, coarse clothes.

Apart from ornaments, people decorated the body with tattoos and natural paint. The colours told you who the person was. Priests were turned out the best. They wore blue. The Maya loved to wear jewellery all over the body, specially on the face, neck, and feet. Ornaments were made of wood, bone, gold, and semi-precious stones like obsidian and jade. Those who wanted more permanent ornamentation had motifs tattooed.

Kings and rich people had their front teeth drilled and filled with stones like jade and obsidian.

The Maya loved headgear and the higher the position of the wearer in society, the taller the hat. Some hats were almost as tall as the person who wore them!

▲ The designs of the headgear differed according to the status of the person.

**and NOW**

Even today, Maya wear many of the clothes like the huipil, and ornaments their ancestors wore hundreds of years ago. Their clothes are still decorated with motifs like the scorpion's tail, the vulture, and the diamond.

16-17

# Reading and writing

The Maya were not the first to figure out how to write, but theirs was the most developed system of writing in Mesoamerica. They had a script in use as early as 300 BC or perhaps even a century earlier. They believed the god Itzamna was the god of writing and of the calendar.

Maya writing looks a little like the ancient Egyptian hieroglyph. So, it is called glyph. Each glyph stood for a sound and a picture. There were more than a thousand glyphs, at least one for each word that the Maya spoke. Since it was difficult to remember so many characters, not more than 500 glyphs were used by one group of people.

▶ The Maya beat the bark of trees into a kind of paper called amatl. Sheets of amatl were folded like an accordion. They recorded so many events that over 10,000 pieces of writing have been found.

Sky  Year  Mountain  Sun  Jaguar  Fire

Bone  Spirit  Book  Water  Lord  Cloud

Woman  To grab  Quetzal  Snake  Holy

So, to write the word for 'sun', the Maya would either have a picture of the sun or the sound symbols that spelled out the words. The writer could use any one or even both ways of describing a word.

Since writing was so important to the Maya, writers or scribes were respected. Not everyone could write. Kings were taught to read and write and they often stuck a pen into their headdress. Many nobles and rich people were illiterate.

Like the Maya religion, customs and language, much of the script fell into disuse when Europeans, particularly the Spanish, took over Mesoamerica. The Spanish conquerors destroyed most of the Maya texts.

▶ Itzamna was an active creator god. The Maya also worshipped him as a priest god who had invented the art of writing.

▶ Maya scribes were artists who used the complex writing system to record important events and activities of rulers.

and NOW

The Maya wrote in books made of bark and plaster. They also carved on monuments, bones, and stone. Many of these writings survive today, and tell us about the Maya civilization.

18-19

Ouch, my tooth hurts!

Hmm...too much of chocolate! But do not worry, we had dentists, too.

# Maya mathemagicians!

The ancient Maya were great mathematicians and scientists. They understood numbers and used them in their writing to describe distance, date or quantity. The primary numbers were zero through twelve. Around 36 BC, they understood the idea of zero. Using numbers, they could work out complicated sums that totalled up to hundreds of millions!

The Maya were brilliant astronomers, too. They studied the planets and made amazingly accurate observations. This also helped them draw up calendars. Astronomers could calculate the day of the week of a date thousands of years in the past or in the future. They could predict events like an eclipse. Although they had no telescopes, they knew of hundreds of stars and understood that the earth went around the sun!

| 0 | 1 | 2 | 3 | 4 |
| 5 | 6 | 7 | 8 | 9 |
| 10 | 11 | 12 | 13 | 14 |

▲ The Maya used a number system in which units were written with dots, and bars were used to represent five units.

5 + 2 = 7

5 + 5 + 5 + 5 + 2 = 22

While one calendar, or almanac, was 260 days long, the sun-based calendar covered 365 days. This helped the Maya draw up a calendar for planting crops rather than leave agriculture to chance.

▲ The Maya studied the movement of the sun and moon to develop more than seventeen calendars, each with a different purpose. One of them, called the 'long count', is a continuous record of days from a zero date that starts from August 13, 3114 BC.

▲ The Maya made medicines from about 1,500 plants. They also knew that stones like jade could be used to treat problems of the kidneys.

Many Maya sites like Monte Alto, La Blanca, and Takalik Abaj were planned to face constellations, or certain groups of stars. Maya scientists studied the movement of the sun and even had a god who they believed helped them work out the time when the sun passed overhead.

Fascinated by the planets, the Maya built observatories to study astronomy. Often, temples were also used as observatories, and their doors were positioned in such a way that astronomers could observe the planets and their movement.

The Maya knew the importance of trees. In the early years, they marked some trees as sacred groves that could not be cut. Priests doubled up as doctors and knew how to fill cavities in teeth, stitch wounds with hair, and mend a fracture. They were also surgeons, cutting unwanted flesh with stone blades.

**and NOW**

The Maya calculated that a year had 365 days—a little short of the time it takes for the earth to move around the sun. Every four years, they missed one day. The modern calendar is more accurate. It has to make up for one day every 3,257 years.

Oh no, look at my clothes!

Hehehe...that's Maya blue, it was made from natural materials, so it won't harm you.

# | Artistic people

The Maya were fond of art. They made and decorated beautiful vases, paintings, and murals. Painters were respected for their art, so they signed off their paintings with glyphs or the typical Maya writing. This was unique to the Mayas, as no other ancient civilization gave the artist so much importance.

Most of the paintings have not survived the ravages of time. The hot, damp climate has damaged most of the art. Some paintings have been spotted on pottery that was used for religious ceremonies and for funerals. One of the few painted murals has been found at Bonampak. The artists painted scenes from daily life, battles, and religious ceremonies.

The Maya sculptor carved out scenes on rocks, stones, and wood. Although they did not have metal tools, the craftsmen were experts at carving hard stones like jade, which they inlaid with other stones like obsidian.

◄ The Maya carved large stone slabs called stelas, showing the rulers of their cities in the form of gods. The hieroglyphic texts on the stelas tell us about the Maya.

GREEN GEM

Maya artists used natural materials in their art—painting on paper and plaster, carvings in wood and stone, clay and stucco models, and terracotta figurines from moulds.

Maya carvings show that they observed the human and animal bodies carefully. Each ruler put up a stone called stela, which was carved with his name and scenes from his life.

The Mayas used many colours in their paintings, but most of the shades have faded away. One colour that shines through the centuries is a bright turquoise blue. It is called Maya blue today. They made this colour out of a clay called palygorskite. Other colours were made from leaves, charcoal, and metals like iron.

▲ Maya artists decorated walls of temples and caves with scenes of battle, ceremonies, and sacrifice. A beautiful turquoise blue colour, called Maya blue, can still be seen in the paintings.

**and NOW**

Although some modern Maya may have turned to other religions, scholars are studying their rituals to understand the religious rites seen in ancient paintings.

# The games they played

Games were an important part of the Maya's life. They were considered a part of religion and a way to honour the gods. They were also used to sort out differences. Every city had ball courts near a temple. Contests were held every twenty days during religious feasts. People came to watch the competitions and sat around on benches built like steps.

The Maya's favourite game was pok-a-tok. It was played in a court with a stone hoop placed at a height of about twenty-three feet at one end. A hard rubber ball had to be passed through this hoop. Pok-a-tok was similar to basketball. It was also something like soccer, as the ball could not be tackled by hand. It could be hit with the shoulders and elbows and even the hips.

Is that basketball or soccer?

That's pok-a-tok, our favourite game.

◀ Music and dance were part of daily life. Processions with large bands of drums and instruments like flutes and rattles were common.

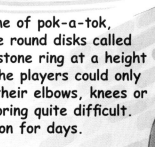

▶ In the Maya game of pok-a-tok, ball courts had three round disks called markers or a single stone ring at a height above the ground. The players could only touch the ball with their elbows, knees or hips, which made scoring quite difficult. The games could go on for days.

**GREEN GEM** The ball game was perhaps a way of worshipping nature. The ball stood for the sun and the game was like its movement.

Since pok-a-tok was a rough game, players wore special clothes to protect themselves. The protective gear included a leather apron, knee pads and elbow pads, chin guards, and cheek guards. Winners kept the jewellery of the losers. Sometimes, undernourished slaves captured from other tribes were made to play against the best players, so that they would lose. The losers—or at least the captain of the losing team—were then sacrificed to keep the gods happy. Some historians believe the winning captain was beheaded by the losing captain, so that he could go straight to heaven!

and NOW

Even today, Ulama, a modern version of the Maya ball game, is played in the land of the Maya.

24-25

# The people and their gods

The Maya were deeply religious people. They worshipped many gods who represented nature. There were gods of rain, lightning, and the sun. Even the rainbow was respected. Since the corn crop was so important, it was worshipped! The Maya built their temples on top of stepped pyramids. With so many gods, there were festivals and celebrations every twenty days.

Priests were important people—it was believed that they could talk to the gods, and they kept the gods happy. They even decided when the corn was to be sown. They also kept in check the demons who lived in the underworld but could creep up to create problems if they were not happy. The underworld was ruled by the gods of death and decay. Sometimes, priests dressed up in animal masks to scare away the demons.

Whoaa, this storm is scary!

That's why we worshipped thunder, lightning, and other things in nature!

▼ The Maya had complex rituals and ceremonies to worship their many gods. Worshippers danced to the music of drums as the priest climbed the steps of temple pyramids to offer sacrifice or drive away demons.

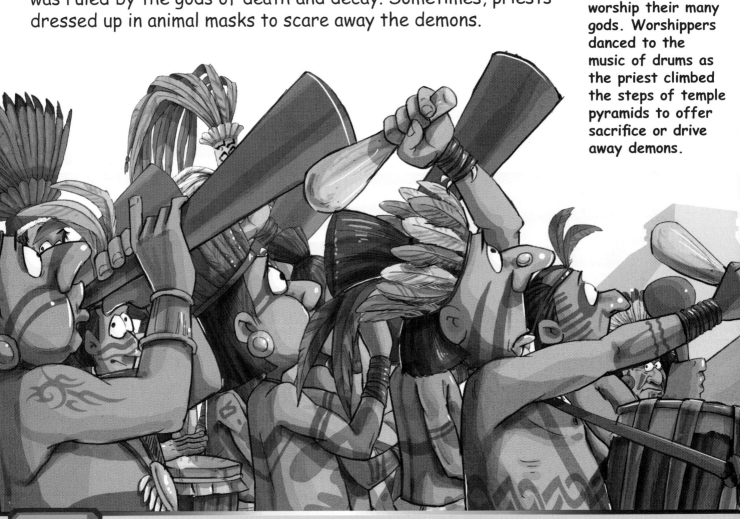

The Maya festivals were linked to the seasons and to nature. They believed crops, especially corn, were a gift from the gods.

The Maya believed that demons could also pop out of mirrors, so only brave men looked into mirrors. As priests went up the pyramids, dancers in headgear danced. They tried to keep the gods happy with sacrifices of animals and people. Sometimes, people just cut or pierced themselves with something sharp. They believed that this would please the gods.

The Maya believed people did not just die. They lived on in an afterlife. So, most people buried their dead family members inside their homes to keep in touch with them. They also believed people were rewarded in their afterlife for any difficulties they suffered in their life. Only kings and nobles were buried in tombs.

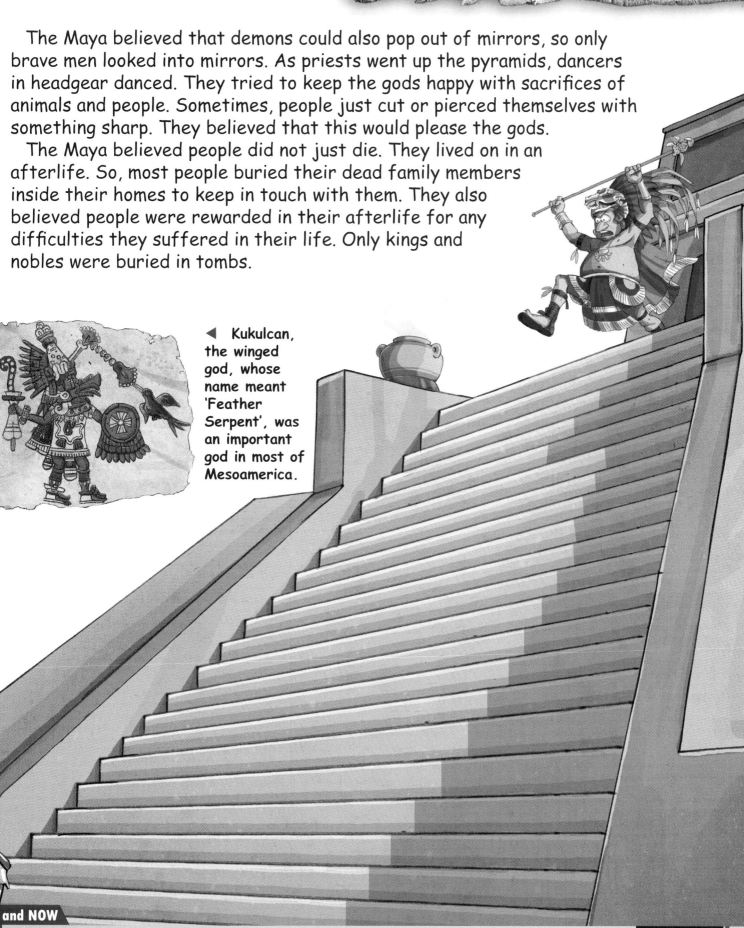

◄ Kukulcan, the winged god, whose name meant 'Feather Serpent', was an important god in most of Mesoamerica.

**and NOW**

Ancient Maya buildings are being discovered even today. In 2001, archaeologists stumbled upon a religious mural in San Bartolo, Guatemala, that tells of the birth of the Maya from the body of the gods.

**26-27**

# Mysterious decline

The ancient Maya were a flourishing civilization from the third to the ninth century. They built magnificent temples and pyramids, and developed highly accurate calendars, mathematics, and hieroglyphic writing. However, between the eighth and ninth centuries, their society seems to have declined and collapsed.

In the powerful and wealthy city of Copán, no monuments seem to have been built after AD 822. Most of the cities of the central lowlands were abandoned at this time, though those in the northern lowlands in Yucatan continued to flourish till the Spanish started conquering Maya lands in the 1520s.

◀ Many historians believe the Maya civilization collapsed due to a series of long droughts lasting several years.

The land that had once been protected by a canopy of trees was exposed to heavy rainfall. Precious soil was washed away. This led to seasons of drought and failed crops.

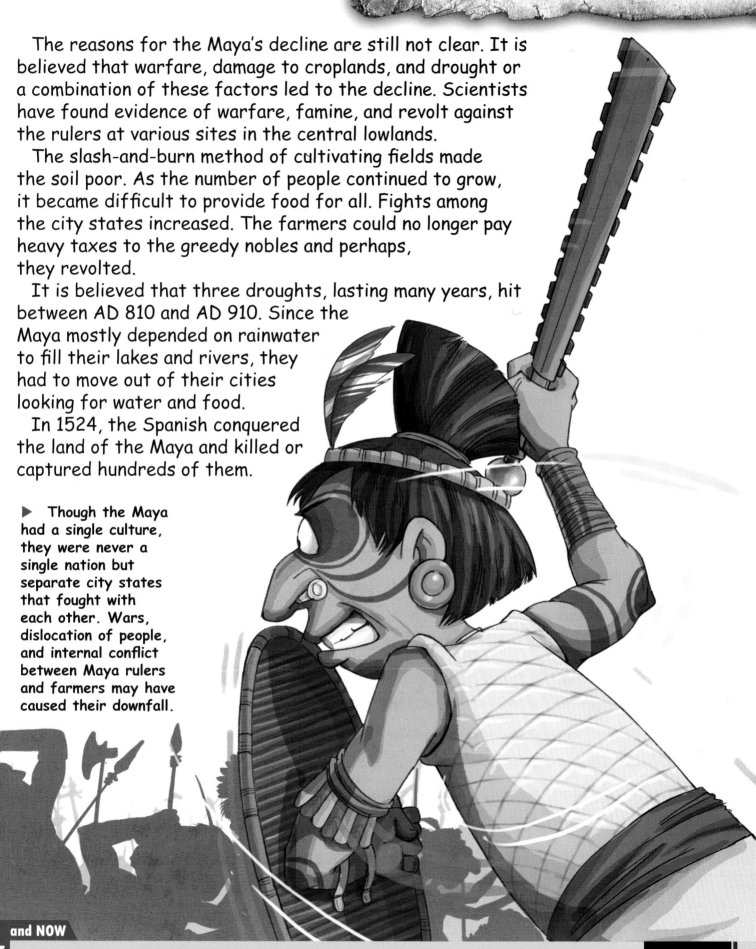

The reasons for the Maya's decline are still not clear. It is believed that warfare, damage to croplands, and drought or a combination of these factors led to the decline. Scientists have found evidence of warfare, famine, and revolt against the rulers at various sites in the central lowlands.

The slash-and-burn method of cultivating fields made the soil poor. As the number of people continued to grow, it became difficult to provide food for all. Fights among the city states increased. The farmers could no longer pay heavy taxes to the greedy nobles and perhaps, they revolted.

It is believed that three droughts, lasting many years, hit between AD 810 and AD 910. Since the Maya mostly depended on rainwater to fill their lakes and rivers, they had to move out of their cities looking for water and food.

In 1524, the Spanish conquered the land of the Maya and killed or captured hundreds of them.

▶ Though the Maya had a single culture, they were never a single nation but separate city states that fought with each other. Wars, dislocation of people, and internal conflict between Maya rulers and farmers may have caused their downfall.

**and NOW**

Even today, there are areas where the Maya live just like their ancestors did, farming corn and living simple lives close to nature.

### Green lessons

- The Maya worked hard to grow food for themselves, and they ate wholesome food that they grew on their land.

- They used innovative methods to grow enough food for their people—like the raised bed method, where permanent raised fields were connected by canals.

- They mixed ash with the soil to make the land more fertile, and caught rainwater in chaltunes, or tanks, lined with plaster.

- They used local material like stone and limestone in their buildings.